Marion Junior High Library
Marion, Arkansas 72364

Property of Marion Junior High School Library

GREAT JOBS

HOME HEALTH AIDE

Ingela Waugh

Marion Junior High Library
Marion, Arkansas 72364

Children's Press®
A Division of Scholastic Inc.
New York / Toronto / London / Auckland / Sydney
Mexico City / New Delhi / Hong Kong
Danbury, Connecticut

Book Design: Christopher Logan and Daniel Hosek
Layout and Production: Mindy Liu
Photo Credits: Cover and p. 36 © Tom Stewart/Corbis; pp. 4, 28 © John Henley/Corbis; p. 7 © Ariel Skelley/Corbis; pp. 8, 11 © Bettmann/Corbis; p. 12 © Hulton-Deutsch Collection/Corbis; p. 15 © Corbis; pp. 16, 34 © Ronnie Kaufman/Corbis; pp. 19, 41 © Paul Barton/Corbis; pp. 21, 23 © Royalty free/Corbis; p. 24 © Michael Pole/Corbis; p. 27 © Don Mason/Corbis; p. 31 © Barros & Barros/Getty Images; p. 33 © Brownie Harris/Corbis; p. 38 © Charles Gupton/Corbis

Library of Congress Cataloging-in-Publication Data

Waugh, Ingela.
  Home health aide / Ingela Waugh.
  p. cm.—(Great jobs)
  Includes bibliographical references and index.
  Contents: Health without hospitals —Trained to help —Taking good care—To your health.
  ISBN 0-516-24087-0 (lib. bdg.) —ISBN 0-516-25934-2 (pbk.)
  1. Home health aides—Juvenile literature. [1. Home health aides—Vocational guidance. 2. Vocational guidance.] I. Title. II. Series.

RA645.3.W38 2003
610.73'43—dc22

2003015392

Copyright © 2004 by Rosen Book Works, Inc. All rights reserved.
Published in 2004 by Children's Press, an imprint of
Scholastic Library Publishing.
Published simultaneously in Canada.
Printed in the United States of America.

CHILDREN'S PRESS and associated logos are trademarks and or registered trademarks of Scholastic Library Publishing. SCHOLASTIC and associated logos are trademarks and or registered trademarks of Scholastic Inc.

1 2 3 4 5 6 7 8 9 10 R 13 12 11 10 09 08 07 06 05 04

Contents

	Introduction	5
1	Health Without Hospitals	9
2	Trained to Help	17
3	Taking Good Care	25
4	To Your Health	37
	New Words	42
	For Further Reading	44
	Resources	45
	Index	47
	About the Author	48

Introduction

The moment Emma arrived at work, she knew that something was wrong. Marco was standing in the doorway, wringing his hands.

"I don't know where Paula is," Marco told Emma. "I just got through changing her bedsheets. She was watching television in the living room. When I finished with the sheets, I went to check on her. She's wandered away."

Emma and Marco are both trained home health aides. Home health aides are trained to help people who cannot take care of themselves. They have many duties. Some help their clients with housework and simple chores. Others may make sure their clients eat properly and take their medication. If the clients are disabled, home health aides help them get from room to room. They make it possible for clients to live in their own homes, instead of hospitals.

> Home health aides like the one pictured here provide their patients with comfort and familiarity.

Emma and Marco's client, Paula, suffers from Alzheimer's disease. This disease slowly destroys a person's memory. People with Alzheimer's can forget where they live, and even forget their own names. Because of their damaged memory, Alzheimer's patients sometimes wander away and become lost.

Quickly, Marco drove to the local police station. At the station, Marco opened a kit that he and Emma had made just for this kind of situation. One of Paula's unwashed shirts is inside this kit. The shirt could help police dogs get Paula's scent and follow her trail. There were also several photos of Paula in the kit.

Meanwhile, Emma took a photo of Paula and walked down the street. She stopped beside a tall office building. Emma took the elevator to the eighth floor. When Emma got off the elevator, she spotted Paula right away. She was standing beside a couch in the lobby. She looked confused and upset.

Paula seemed to recognize Emma, but she did not say anything. Because of her disease, Paula hardly ever spoke.

> Patients who hire home health aides have usually reached the point where they need daily medical assistance.

Introduction

Emma came over to Paula and comforted her. "You came to your old office," she explained. Long ago, Paula had told Emma about working in this building. For twenty years, Paula had worked as an accountant here. "You don't work here anymore, Paula," Emma continued. "It's time to come home."

Home health aides have to understand their clients' feelings. They must earn their clients' trust. Also, they have to be prepared for medical problems and emergencies. This makes their job a demanding one. However, as this book shows, home health aides receive many rewards. They make peoples' lives richer and fuller. Home health aides can sometimes even save lives.

CHAPTER ONE

Health Without Hospitals

These days, very sick or injured people often go to hospitals. They expect to find the best care there. However, in the late nineteenth century, hospitals did not always have a good reputation. Many of them were dirty. The hospital workers were often not well trained. If a family member got sick, that person usually stayed at home. If sick people had enough money, they would pay for private doctors to care for them. Otherwise, the family would provide the care. Many ill people only went to hospitals as a last resort.

At this time, many immigrants were coming to the United States. An immigrant is someone who comes from abroad to live permanently in a country. Immigrants often arrived in the United States with little money in their pockets. They usually had

The visiting nurse movement paved the way for advances in the field of home health care. Nurses like these served the poor communities in New York City's Lower East Side.

to deal with awful living conditions. This made it easy for them to catch infectious diseases. An infectious disease is an illness that spreads quickly.

When poor people caught infectious diseases, there was little they could do. They couldn't afford private doctors, so their death rates were very high. These sick people needed trained health care workers who could come to their homes.

Agencies of Change

Home care agencies were started to fill this need. The agencies sent visiting nurses into the homes of sick people.

Visiting nurses had many duties. They taught family members the best way to care for one another. They advised people on a number of important hygiene lessons. By putting these lessons into action, immigrants stayed healthier. Fewer germs spread in cities and towns. This helped slow the growth of dangerous diseases.

> Visiting nurses tried to learn whether or not their clients were keeping up with basic hygiene.

Health Without Hospitals

Visiting nurses also cared for people with chronic illnesses. A chronic illness, such as diabetes, cannot be spread. However, people suffering from them may have to fight their illnesses for their entire lives.

Not all of a visiting nurse's duties involved helping sick people. The nurses also helped deliver babies. They also helped new mothers learn how to care for their babies. They gave them tips on how to protect infants from illness.

Around 1910, a visiting nurse named Lillian Wald made a powerful argument about the important nature of her profession. Wald promised insurance companies that they could save big money by hiring visiting nurses.

Each year, customers paid money to insurance companies. When a customer died, the company

Health Without Hospitals

> After World War I, many wounded soldiers received care from American Red Cross nurses.

gave money to the customer's family. Wald pointed out that visiting nurses often kept sick people alive longer. Each year a customer lives, he or she would continue to pay money to the company. This meant that the company would receive more payments from each customer.

Wald's good points convinced Metropolitan Life. This insurance company decided to offer visiting nurse services to all their customers.

The visiting nurse movement grew by leaps and bounds. From 1914 to 1920, sixty-eight Red Cross visiting nurse programs opened every month! People had become convinced that visiting nurses improved patients' lives.

TAKING CARE OF BUSINESS

Some nurses actually lived in the homes of wealthy patients. They were on duty 24 hours a day.

Peaks and Valleys

Around 1925, the home nursing movement began to slow down. Several visiting nurse programs were forced to end. Scientists were finding cures for infectious diseases. New hospitals were being built. The conditions and services inside these hospitals had greatly improved. Patients who were pregnant or needed surgery began to seek out hospital care.

By the 1960s, home health care began to grow again. People were living longer. The number of hospital stays that each person made increased. While hospital care was still very good, its costs were growing. To save money, patients would only want to stay in the hospital for short periods. Once they were well enough, they would go home. The patients then paid for cheaper private care while they finished healing.

In the 1960s, the U.S. Congress began to get involved with home health care. It saw the value in caring for ill, elderly, and disabled people in their own homes. Home care made patients feel

During his presidency, Lyndon Johnson (shown here) improved health care for the elderly through a program called Medicare.

Health Without Hospitals

more comfortable. It was often cheaper for the patients, as well. Congress passed laws that required the government to help pay for many types of home care. They do this through programs such as Medicare and Medicaid.

Home care remains a vital part of health services in the United States. In 1992, the federal government made an important discovery. They found that home care was the second-fastest-growing industry in the nation. They predicted that half a million new home care jobs would be created between 1992 and 2005.

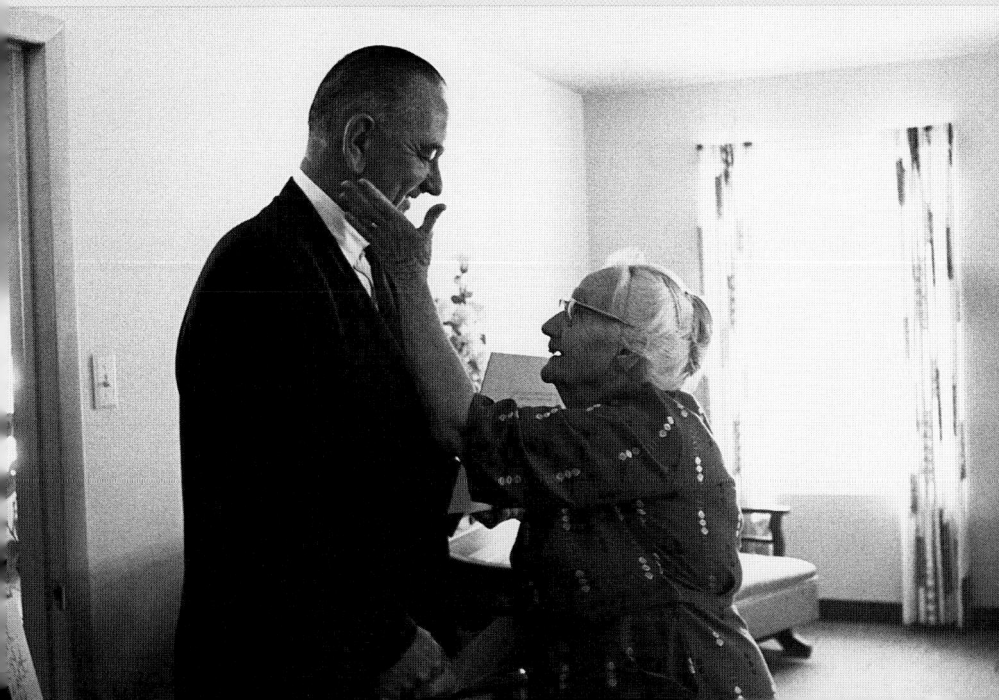

CHAPTER TWO

Trained to Help

Many different types of health professionals travel to patients' homes to care for them. This includes more than 200,000 home health aides working in the United States. It also includes health care workers known as therapists. They are trained to treat special problems. For instance, physical therapists treat patients suffering from, or disabled by, injuries. Another kind of therapist helps those patients who have speech problems. Many of these clients are recovering from strokes, which often harm someone's ability to speak.

In most cases, people who strive to become home health aides must graduate from a training course. These courses are offered at many community colleges, universities, and medical schools. The courses

Part of a home health aide's job is to make sure that his or her clients continue to lead active lives.

> In the event of a medical emergency, all home health aides are trained to measure their patients' vital signs.

usually involve about 60 hours in the classroom. They also involve 16 hours in a lab or a clinic.

During their training programs, future home health aides learn how to keep germs from spreading in a client's home. They learn basic nursing skills, such as how to measure and record a client's vital signs. Vital signs are signals of how healthy a person is. They include measurements such as blood pressure, heart rate, and body temperature.

Home health aides learn about nutrition and healthy eating. They learn how to record the kinds of care that the patient has received. They also learn what to do in the event of a medical emergency.

Many clients have trouble with even the simplest forms of personal care. They often have great diffi-

TAKING CARE OF BUSINESS

There are more than twenty thousand home care agencies in the United States. Aides working for these agencies help care for more than seven million people each year.

culty walking, bathing, or simply getting out of bed. Training programs teach aides how to help move their clients safely. For instance, lifting patients out of bed improperly can lead to serious injuries. Safe lifting can prevent back spasms and pulled muscles.

Patience With Patients

Home health aides often work with mentally ill or disabled clients. Other clients may suffer from Alzheimer's disease or have had strokes. Sometimes these types of clients have trouble expressing themselves. Their frustration may lead to mood swings or unpleasant behavior. They may try to prevent home health aides from doing their duties. Training programs teach methods that help aides deal with uncooperative clients.

Other clients may be mentally alert. However, they may be in so much physical pain that they can no longer complete simple tasks. They may take out their anger on the aides trying to help them. Some wind up insulting their aides, or even growing violent with them.

Often the most effective way to deal with this type of client is through careful listening. If a client has an outburst of anger, the health aide must remain patient. Aides have to remember that a client's anger is not a personal attack. Usually the patient is scared, confused, or depressed. By remaining good-natured and generous, home health aides often improve their clients' moods. If a home health aide can keep the spirits of their clients high, it will make their job go much more smoothly. Aides are at their best when they encourage their clients to remain as active and positive as possible.

Part of a home health aide's day is often devoted to helping out with household chores, such as cooking meals.

License to Heal

At the end of the training program, home health aides must pass a written exam. Once they have passed, they are ready to apply for state licenses. Each home health aide must get a license from the state in which he or she lives. There is usually an application fee of about $70 for the license.

After aides get their licenses, they often work for home care agencies. These agencies match aides with clients. A trainer or registered nurse will often supervise a home health aide's work.

An Aide's Helpful Tools

Depending on their clients' strength and mobility, home health aides may need to use special equipment on the job.

One piece of special equipment is called a transfer board. Transfer boards are used to help clients move back and forth from their beds to their wheelchairs. They are made from flat pieces of wood or plastic. The board has handles cut into either end of it.

A home health aide places one end of the transfer board on the wheelchair seat. The other end is placed on the bed's edge. Using their hands, clients push across the transfer board. If the client cannot push him- or herself, aides sometimes use a hydraulic lift.

Home health aides may use other special equipment. For instance, some clients rely on oxygen tanks to help them breathe. Other clients depend on special seats to help them take showers. Aides may also need to know how to use wheelchairs and artificial limbs.

> Many elderly patients rely on walkers, wheelchairs, transfer boards, and other devices to help keep them mobile.

Trained to Help

• TAKING CARE OF BUSINESS

The U.S. Department of Labor lists the home health aide field as the fastest-growing health care profession in the United States.

CHAPTER THREE

Taking Good Care

Selma's Story
Home health aides usually have to assist several clients each day. This chapter follows a fictional home health care aide named Selma. The chapter charts Selma's long workday, which stretches from dawn until dusk.

Leo
Selma's first patient of the day is also her youngest. Her patient's name is Leo. Selma is due to arrive at his apartment at 8 A.M.

Leo is twenty-five years old. A few months ago, he was in a terrible car accident. He was involved in a head-on collision with another car. His legs were badly injured in the crash. Leo, however, was the lucky one. The other driver died instantly after the collision.

> Home health aides help their clients' emotional states as well as their physical states. They are often called upon to cheer up sad or angry clients.

During Selma's visits, she cooks breakfast for Leo and tidies up his apartment. She washes the dishes, vacuums, and changes Leo's bedsheets. Selma also keeps Leo as physically active as she can. She helps Leo stretch his legs to regain flexibility. Leo's doctors believe that he will be able to walk again within one year. Selma will continue to assist Leo, at least until that day arrives.

When Selma arrives at Leo's apartment today, she finds him lying on the living room floor. She rushes to help him. She checks his vital signs and makes sure he is conscious. Conscious means to be aware of your surroundings.

"Leo," Selma asks, "what happened here?"

"I fell asleep watching the morning news on television," Leo says. "Next thing I know, I was tumbling out of my wheelchair."

Using the lifting techniques she had learned during her training program, Selma picks Leo up off the floor. She carefully places him back in his wheelchair.

> Some health care professionals are physical therapists. Their job is to help clients recover from bad experiences, such as car accidents.

Taking Good Care

Selma says, "Leo, you didn't fasten your seat belt."

"I didn't feel like it," Leo grumbles.

"Leo, you have to buckle your seat belt to prevent accidents. You could've gotten a serious head injury."

"So what if I did?" Leo says angrily.

"Selma, last year at this time, I had a job in construction. I was playing basketball on the weekends. Now I can't do anything. I can't even get up off the floor on my own. I have to face facts—it's no use trying. I'm never going to leave this wheelchair."

Selma has seen Leo have outbursts like this before. She knows that he sometimes grows depressed over his injury. However, she has built a great relationship with Leo, so she knows how to calm him down. "It's natural to be upset," she tells him. "You need to remember that you're making progress. Each time you stretch and exercise, you get a little closer to walking again. Besides, I know you've told me how lucky you were that you weren't killed in that accident." As Selma talks, Leo's mood brightens. By the time she's done, he's eager to work on his exercises.

Kevin

After Selma helps Leo, she takes a bus across town. She is headed to see her second patient of the day, Kevin. Kevin is seventy-six years old. He is partially

> Some frustrated patients just need a gentle push from their home health aides in order to enjoy life again.

blind and has diabetes. Diabetes is a disease in which there is too much sugar in the body's blood.

Selma arrives at Kevin's house at 1 P.M. Kevin lives with his son Gregory. Gregory appreciates Selma's help. He is the manager of a restaurant that stays open late. Without Selma, Gregory would have a difficult time caring for his father. Once Selma arrives, Gregory can leave for his job without worrying about his father. Selma leaves at 4 P.M. That's when Gregory's wife comes back home from her job.

Selma begins her time with Kevin by preparing a special meal for him. Soon after that, it's time for Kevin's insulin injection. Insulin is a chemical hormone that regulates the amount of sugar in a person's body. Insulin helps to manage diabetes. An important part of Selma's job is to give Kevin this insulin injection. Thanks to her training, Selma knows exactly how to complete this delicate procedure.

Next, Selma takes Kevin for a walk in the park. This allows Kevin to get some exercise. It's one of

> Home health aides are trained to be able to give injections and correct dosages of medicine.

Selma's favorite parts of the day. Kevin seems to know every flower in the park. He teaches Selma everything about the flowers, from their names to their growing habits.

Carol and Bob

In late afternoon, Selma heads to Carol's house. Carol is Selma's last patient of the day. Carol is seventy-nine years old. She has breast cancer. To treat her breast cancer, Carol is taking chemotherapy. Chemotherapy is a treatment using chemicals that can kill the diseased cells in cancer patients.

Although Carol is still an active woman, the chemotherapy has made her weak. Carol's husband, Bob, takes care of his wife when he can. However, Bob is elderly, too. He doesn't always have the strength to assist Carol.

Each day, Selma takes Carol's temperature and blood pressure. She helps her shower and dress. Selma does the laundry and dishes for both Bob and Carol.

> Some patients are taken by their home health aides to social functions where they can interact with friends.

Selma also drives Carol downtown twice a week to attend a special class. This class is filled with people who are also surviving cancer. It makes Carol feel stronger knowing that there are other people going through the same disease she is.

The Day's Last Stop

Selma has finished up with Bob and Carol. That means it's time for her to drop by her health care agency. Selma reports to her supervisor. She also speaks with doctors, therapists, nurses, and dieticians. Selma lets all these health care professionals know how her patients are doing.

Selma's clients are usually grateful for her help and compassion. Thanks to Selma, they can live at home instead of in a hospital. Selma has developed a special relationship with her clients. She has worked with some of them, such as Kevin, for many years. Others, like Leo, will only need her help for a short time. To Selma, working in other people's homes is more comfortable than working in an office or a factory.

Being a home health aide can be hard work. Most of Selma's workdays last for at least twelve hours. Despite the job's difficulties, Selma always looks forward to going to work in the morning. She knows she is making a difference. She knows she is helping people to have better, happier lives.

> The best home health aides brighten their patients' lives with each visit. They do more than assist their patients—they improve their lives.

CHAPTER FOUR

To Your Health

A Growing Need

Home health care in the United States is a fast-growing industry. It's easy to see why. More and more people in this country have longer life spans. As they age, they need assistance to go about their daily routines. Most elderly Americans who need this assistance simply cannot afford to stay in hospitals. They also prefer to be cared for in their homes, which feel more comfortable and familiar to them. Hospitals are often overcrowded and many doctors have too many patients as it is. Home health aides ease this burden.

The Next Stage?

The hours that home health aides are expected to work may be long and difficult. Since patients need

> Americans are living longer life spans than ever before. If this trend continues, the role of home health aides will become even more important.

Home Health Aide

health assistance around the clock, most home health aides work on weekends as well as weekdays. There is often a great deal of driving or traveling involved with their job. After all, aides don't have a single office to go to. They must travel from home to home.

TAKING CARE OF BUSINESS

Experienced home health aides earn about $10 an hour. Their annual salary can range from $10,000 to over $35,000.

There are not many ways for a home health aide to advance his or her career. However, aides who are very good at their jobs do have some options.

For example, a home health aide may become self-employed. By doing this, they will work for themselves instead of working through an agency. This will allow them to set their own hours. It will also allow them to charge their own fees. However, they will no longer have an agency matching them up with patients. Self-employed home health aides will need to find clients on their own. Self-employed aides need to have ambition and energy if they wish to succeed.

Experienced home health aides could also become supervisors or specialists. Both of these positions command a higher salary than that of an aide.

Some home health aides go on to become specialists. They may treat patients, such as this child, that require special needs.

A specialist knows about a specific area of home health care, such as the use of medical equipment. Supervisors monitor the work of home health aides. They may make around $20 an hour.

Career Move

After a few years of experience, home health aides may choose to move into a related career. For example, an aide could take classes to become a home health nurse. While nurses have higher salaries than home health aides, they definitely have more responsibilities. To become a nurse, aides must be willing to go through about two to three years worth of training and education.

Home health aides are caring, kind, and have a great desire to help people. Good home health aides know that they make their patients feel more relaxed and more at ease. They get satisfaction from their jobs because they know that they help make peoples' lives better.

> By enriching their patients' lives, home health aides help make an important difference in the world.

NEW WORDS

Alzheimer's disease (**awlts**-hye-muhrz duh-**zeez**) a disease of the nervous system that damages brain cells, causing problems with memory and judgment

chemotherapy (kee-moh-**ther**-uh-pee) the use of chemicals to kill diseased cells in cancer patients

diabetes (dye-uh-**bee**-teez) a disease in which there is too much sugar in the blood

hygiene (**hye**-jeen) actions taken by people to stay healthy and keep clean

immigrant (**im**-uh-gruhnt) someone who comes from abroad to live permanently in a country

infectious disease (in-**fek**-shuhss duh-**zeez**) a disease that can spread from one person to another by germs or viruses in the air or on objects

insulin (**in**-suh-luhn) a hormone produced in the pancreas that regulates the amount of sugar that you have in your body

NEW WORDS

insurance (in-**shu**-ruhnss) an agreement where a person pays money to a company; this company then agrees to pay the person in the event of sickness, fire, accident, or other loss

mobility (**moh**-bil-i-tee) the ability to move around on one's own

registered nurse (**rej**-uh-sturd **nurss**) a nurse who has completed certain training and is licensed by the state in which he or she practices

specialist (**spesh**-uh-list) an expert at one particular job or area

therapist (**ther**-uh-pist) someone who treats an illness, injury, or disability

transfer board (transs-**fur bord**) flat pieces of wood or plastic used to transport patients

vital signs (**vye**-tuhl **sines**) signs of life, such as pulse rate, body temperature, and blood pressure

FOR FURTHER READING

Pasternak, Ceel and Linda Thornburg. *Cool Careers for Girls in Health*. Manassas Park, VA: Impact Publications, 1999.

Quinlan, Kathryn A. *Nurse Assistant*. Mankato, MN: Capstone Press, Inc., 1998.

Simon, Charnan. *Home Health Aide*. Mankato, MN: Capstone Press, Inc., 1998.

RESOURCES

Organizations

Home Care Association of America, Inc.
9570 Regency Square Boulevard
Jacksonville, FL 32225

National Association for Home Care
228 7th Street, SE
Washington, DC 20003
(202) 547-7424

World Homecare and Hospice Organization
228 7th Street, SE
Washington, DC 20003
(202) 546-4756

RESOURCES

Web Sites

Homecare Online
www.nahc.org
This Web site provides plenty of facts about home health care. It even provides some job and agency information.

BLS Career Information — Registered Nurse
www.bls.gov/k12/html/sci_004.htm
Viewers of this Web site can learn about what nurses do, their pay scale, and the future of the job. The site also provides addresses and organizations you can contact to receive further news updates and information.

INDEX

A
agencies, 10, 21
Alzheimer's disease, 6, 19

C
chemotherapy, 32
chronic illness, 11
clients, 5, 7, 17–22, 25, 35, 39

D
diabetes, 11, 30
disabled, 5, 14, 17, 19
disease, 6, 10, 19, 30, 33
duties, 5, 10, 12, 20

E
emergency, 18

G
germs, 10, 18

H
hospitals, 5, 9, 14, 37
housework, 5
hygiene, 10

I
immigrant, 9
infectious disease, 10
insulin, 30
insurance, 12–13

K
kit, 6

L
license, 21

M
Medicaid, 15
Medicare, 15
medication, 5
Metropolitan Life, 13
mobility, 22
mood swings, 19–20

INDEX

N
nutrition, 18

R
Red Cross, 13
registered nurse, 21
rewards, 7

S
specialist, 40
strokes, 17, 19
supervisor, 35

T
therapist, 17
transfer board, 22

V
visiting nurses, 10–13
vital signs, 18, 26

W
Wald, Lillian, 12
wheelchair, 22, 26, 29

About the Author
Ingela Waugh enjoys volunteering at her local hospital. She lives in upstate New York with her dog and two parakeets. She enjoys hiking and kayaking.

Marion Junior High Library
Marion, Arkansas 72364